BOY, WERE WE WRONG
ABOUT
DINOSAURS!

Kathleen V. Kudlinski · ILLUSTRATED BY S. D. Schindler

DUTTON CHILDREN'S BOOKS · NEW YORK

DUTTON CHILDREN'S BOOKS

A division of Penguin Young Readers Group

Published by the Penguin Group

Penguin Group (USA) Inc., 375 Hudson Street, New York, New York 10014, U.S.A. • Penguin Group (Canada), 10 Alcorn Avenue, Toronto, Ontario, Canada M4V 3B2 (a division of Pearson Penguin Canada Inc.) • Penguin Books Ltd, 80 Strand, London WC2R 0RL, England • Penguin Ireland, 25 St Stephen's Green, Dublin 2, Ireland (a division of Penguin Books Ltd) • Penguin Group (Australia), 250 Camberwell Road, Camberwell, Victoria 3124, Australia (a division of Pearson Australia Group Pty Ltd) • Penguin Books India Pvt Ltd, 11 Community Centre, Panchsheel Park, New Delhi—110 017, India • Penguin Group (NZ), Cnr Airborne and Rosedale Roads, Albany, Auckland 1310, New Zealand (a division of Pearson New Zealand Ltd) • Penguin Books (South Africa) (Pty) Ltd, 24 Sturdee Avenue, Rosebank, Johannesburg 2196, South Africa • Penguin Books Ltd, Registered Offices: 80 Strand, London WC2R 0RL, England

Library of Congress Cataloging-in-Publication Data

Kudlinski, Kathleen V.

Boy, were we wrong about dinosaurs!/by Kathleen V. Kudlinski; illustrated by S.D. Schindler.—1st ed.

p. cm.

Summary: Examines what is known about dinosaur bones, behavior, and other characteristics and how different the facts often are from what scientists, from ancient China to the recent past, believed to be true. Includes bibliographical references.

ISBN 0-525-46978-8

1. Dinosaurs—Juvenile literature. [1. Dinosaurs. 2. Science—History. 3. Errors, Popular.] I. Schindler, S.D., ill. II. Title.

QE861.5.K84 2005

567.9—dc22   2003053140

Published in the United States by Dutton Children's Books,

a division of Penguin Young Readers Group

345 Hudson Street, New York, New York 10014

www.penguin.com/youngreaders

Manufactured in China • First Edition

3 5 7 9 10 8 6 4 2

To the Toddy Pond Writers,
Doe Boyle, Leslie Bulion, Mary-Kelly Busch, Leslie Connor,
Lorraine Jay, Judy Theise, Nancy Antle, and Nancy Elizabeth Wallace

K.V.K.

LONG, LONG AGO, before people knew anything about dinosaurs, giant bones were found in China. Wise men who saw the bones tried to guess what sort of enormous animal they could have come from.

After they studied the fossil bones, the ancient Chinese decided that they came from dragons. They thought these dragons must have been magic dragons to be so large. And they believed that dragons could still be alive.

Boy, were they wrong!

No one knows exactly what dinosaurs looked like. All that is left of them are fossil bones and a few other clues. Now we think that many of our own past guesses about dinosaurs were just as wrong as those of ancient China.

Some of our mistakes were little ones. When the first fossil bones of *Iguanodon* were found, one was shaped like a rhino's horn. Scientists guessed that the strange bone fit like a spike on *Iguanodon*'s nose.

Boy, were we wrong about *Iguanodon!*

When a full set of fossil bones was found later, there were *two* pointed bones.

They were part of *Iguanodon*'s hands, not its nose!

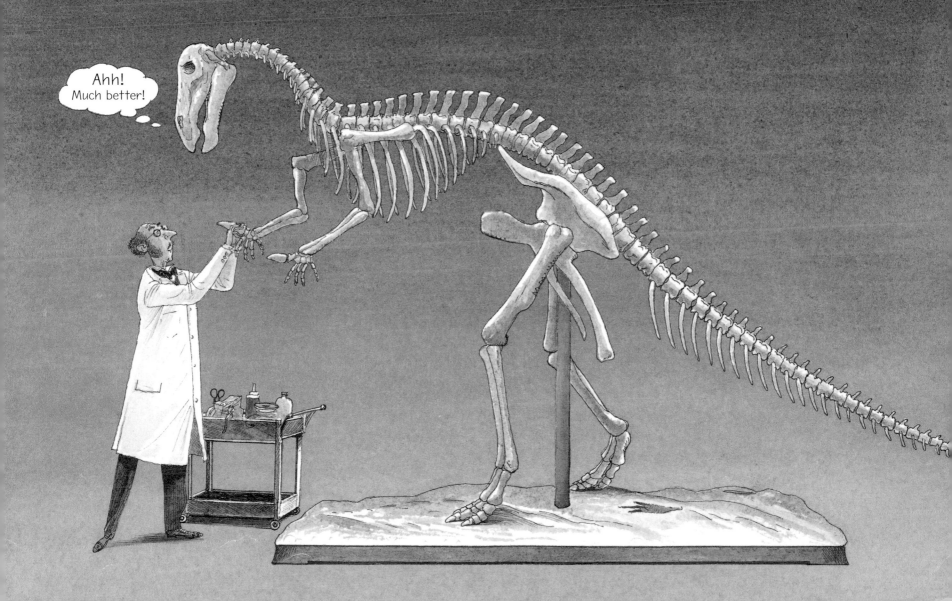

Other new clues show us that we may have been wrong about every kind of dinosaur.

Some of our first drawings of dinosaurs showed them with their elbows and knees pointing out to the side, like a lizard's. With legs like that, big dinosaurs could only waddle clumsily on all fours or float underwater.

Now we know their legs were straight under them, like a horse's. Dinosaurs were not clumsy. The sizes and shapes of their leg bones seem to show that some were as fast and graceful as deer.

Paintings in old books show dinosaurs dragging their tails in the dirt because a few fossils of tail drags were found. And scientists couldn't imagine how muscles could hold up the enormous tails.

Dinosaurs may have been more like birds, with bodies that were warm and full of energy, night and day. They would have needed this extra energy to move their graceful legs.

Are we right about dinosaurs yet? Now some scientists think they were neither cold-blooded nor warm-blooded, but something in between. There is no way to be sure.

Scientists used to think all dinosaurs were scaly, because a few fossil skins showed bumps that look like scales. Now more fossils have been found with marks that seem to be from feathers. What did dinosaurs have on their skin: bumps, scales, or feathers? We can only guess, but we have some good ideas.

Because big animals lose heat more slowly, we think that the big dinosaurs, like the big elephants of today, wouldn't have needed fur or feathers to keep themselves warm.

In the last few years, fossils of many kinds of little dinosaurs have been found. Some grew no bigger than pigeons. These small animals needed some way to keep from losing their body heat. Some of the fossils show warm, fluffy feathers like a baby chick's. Others show long feathers like a rooster's.

Scientists used to think that large dinosaurs were gray, like today's gray elephants. But if that were true, bigger meat-eating dinosaurs would be able to see these gray dinosaurs against colorful leaves and grasses, and they would be eaten. Now scientists think that dinosaurs had colorful patterns that protected them from being found and eaten. Colors and patterns also probably helped dinosaurs show their sex and age to other dinosaurs, the way birds do.

Recent X-rays of some dinosaur fossils show that they had birdlike skulls, with room for large eyes and enough brain space for color vision.

We used to think that dinosaur mothers acted like lizard mothers. Boy, were we wrong! Lizards just lay their eggs on the ground, then leave. They never see their own babies.

Now we have found fossil dinosaur eggs in fossil nests. Some of the nests hold newly hatched babies. Other nests are packed tightly with older baby dinosaurs. These youngsters have scratches on their teeth from eating tough plants. Did their mothers bring food back to the nest? Or did the young go out to feed, then come back home to sleep? We can only guess, but these are things that lizards never do.

In one place, many nests of fossil dinosaur eggs have been found on a hill. It must have been a safe place, because different kinds of dinosaur mothers made their nests there year after year.

Fossil footprints have been found that show a whole herd of dinosaurs walking together. Footprints of baby dinosaurs are there, too, walking safely in the middle of the herd. So we know some dinosaurs took good care of their babies.

Even our ideas about the end of the dinosaurs seem to have been wrong. Scientists used to think that the world slowly dried out or got hotter and that heat and disease killed every dinosaur.

In the last few years, we have found a fossil layer of dust that is probably from outer space. This new clue makes us think a comet or asteroid might have hit the Earth and exploded, setting off fires and tidal waves. It could have made a huge dust cloud that would have poisoned the rain and blocked the sunshine for years.

Most plants can't grow without sunlight. And acid rain makes plants and animals weak and sick. If the plants all died, the animals that ate those plants couldn't find food. And if those animals died, the meat-eaters wouldn't have any food, either.

Scientists think all this might have happened before the cloud settled to a thick layer of dust on the earth. But we could still be wrong about the end of the dinosaurs.

TERTIARY

CRETACEOUS

ASH LAYER

In one way, the scientists of today agree with the Chinese of long ago. They believe some dinosaurs are still alive. Toward the end of the millions and millions of years that dinosaurs lived on Earth, some of the smaller, feathered kinds changed bit by bit. Over the years, their feathers became longer. They began to fly. Gradually, they became birds. While the rest of the dinosaurs died out, somehow some of these birds survived. If scientists are right, our birds are living dinosaurs.

There are still dinosaur books in libraries and bookstores that show the old ways of thinking. Scientists keep finding new clues, and our thinking has to change. Perhaps today's ideas about dinosaurs will someday seem just as silly as the magic dragons of long-ago China.

When you grow up, you may be the scientist who makes us all say, "Boy, were we wrong about dinosaurs!"

A DINOSAUR DISCOVERY TIMELINE

1822   Gideon Mantell, a British doctor, names an ancient animal *Iguanodon*.

1842   Richard Owen, an English anatomist and paleontologist, comes up with the term *Dinosauria*, or "great reptile."

1923   Explorer Roy Chapman Andrews finds dinosaur eggs in the Gobi Desert.

1964   Paleontologist John H. Ostrom questions the cold-bloodedness of dinosaurs.

1968   Paleontologist Robert Bakker draws dinosaurs standing straight with tails upheld.

1973   John H. Ostrom says birds are dinosaurs.

1970's   Walter Alvarez, a geologist, discovers a thin layer of iridium dust.

1978   Jack Horner finds dinosaur nests with fossil young still in them.

1999   Xiao-Chun Wu and Mark Norell both find feathered dinosaur fossils in China.

WHERE YOU CAN DIG FOR MORE INFORMATION

Norman, David, et al. *Eyewitness: Dinosaurs*. New York: DK Publishing, 2000.
Basic dinosaur facts and photos of fossils.

Lambert, David, et al. *Dinosaur Encyclopedia: From Dinosaurs to the Dawn of Man*. New York: DK Publishing, 2001. Answers every possible question on the subject.

A FEW OF THE WORKS USED IN THE RESEARCH FOR THIS BOOK

Farlow, James, and M.K. Brett-Surman, eds. *The Complete Dinosaur*. Bloomington, IN: Indiana University Press, 1997.

Horner, John. *Digging Dinosaurs*. New York: Workman Publishing Company, 1988.

Lucas, Spencer G. *Dinosaurs: The Textbook*. New York: McGraw-Hill Professional Publishing, 1996.

THANKS TO THE SCIENTISTS WHO HELPED IN THE WRITING OF THIS BOOK

Daniel Lee Brinkman, Peabody Museum of Natural History, Yale University.

Byron Butler, Peabody Museum of Natural History, Yale University.

Mark Norell, chairman and curator, Division of Paleontology, American Museum of Natural History, New York City.